To: delnora

Happy memories

Edward keller

Merry Christmas 8-6-04

To Ben from Grt Grandma Delnora

# *My First Grade, 1932*

*by*
*Dr. Edward Keller*

## Dedication

I dedicate this book to the memory of my kind and loving immigrant German from Russia father, Frank M. Keller, who never had an opportunity to go to any school, yet gave so much that I could go to school.

I also dedicate this book to all the teachers who taught me at Wells School #18: Mrs. Orin Wells, Miss Rosina Vetter, Miss Mamie McGee, Miss Mary Eva Vetter and Mr. Levi Kruschwoods.

Dr. Edward Keller

## Preface

"My First Grade, 1932" is a story about Dr. Keller's
first grade on their early Dakota prairie farm.
The time is the 1930s in Strasburg, North Dakota.

Keller creates a memory story of his first year
at school in a one room school house.

# *My First Grade, 1932*

*by*
*Dr. Edward Keller*

*illustrations by David Christy*

© David Christy 2003

At my Strasburg,

North Dakota

rural school in

1932,

Miss Wells, the slender, dark, pretty teacher

with a spit curl crossing her forehead,

says I can start school at age 5, because I have sisters and brothers: Frank, Debert, Wilma and Mary to watch for me.

© David Christy 2003

We drive the three miles in
a sled or buggy with Dave
and Tootsy.

As we pass through Hagel's farm we pick up Martha, a pretty girl with a light face and light hair.

When we are almost to school
we pass through Klein's farm
and Maggie, Rose and Joe
Klein join our ride.

© David Christy 2003

Klein's mother is my godmother and pays
attention to me and encourages Tootsy and
Dave and I feel happy…

At school the team has its very own stall in
the red barn and eats the hay we sat on.

Joe, John, Helen and Frank
Kuhn also come with a team
smaller and faster than
Dave and Tootsy.

Tony Kelsch rides his pony, Spike.

Jake, Joe and Mary Horner walk their mile unless the weather is

too cold, then their older brother, Peter, takes them in a sled.

© David Christy 2003

Joe Vetter walks

his half mile to

school.

To get warm before classes I gather with all the students around the red hot stove.

The smell of coal, varnish and earlier barn chores permeate the room.

Miss Wells starts the

school day by hanging

a flag on a little pole

against the outside of

the school,

© David Christy 2003

and then ringing

a hand bell.

Singing is the first of the 15 minute class sessions.
"My Country Tis of Thee", "Old Black Joe",

"Old MacDonald Had a Farm" and
"Carry Me Back To Old Virginie" fill the room.

Class sessions at the front of the
room are recitals and teacher talk.

During eighth
grade Agriculture
I hear about
Leghorns,
Plymouth Rocks,
Guernseys,
Holsteins,
Percherons and
Belgians.

© David Christy 2003

Fifth grade Geography is about
Bismarck, North Dakota... Pierre,
South Dakota and Sacramento,
California.

Pierre, South Dakota

Bismarck
North Dakota

Sacramento, California

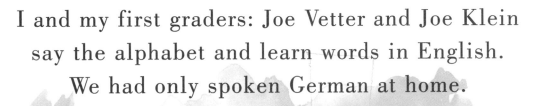

I and my first graders: Joe Vetter and Joe Klein
say the alphabet and learn words in English.
We had only spoken German at home.

Then it is time for a 15 minute recess and a fox and geese game in the snow.

More classes and then lunch hour follows.

Everyone eats at their desk.

Miss Wells has lettuce sandwiches and drinks from a black thermos.

Martha has a blue lunch box and thermos with orange nectar. She shares bites of her jelly bread and pieces of chicken with me… a welcome complement to my syrup sandwiches from an empty syrup pail.

© David Christy 2003

Tony Kelsch enjoys hard boiled eggs
and syrup sandwiches.

The Kuhn children have cream with
sprinkled sugar sandwiches.

Joe Vetter loves sausages from
the night before and plain bread.

The Horner's too have syrup sandwiches.

I watch Mary Horner eat.

She is the prettiest one in school.

During lunch hour
I play at Beaver
Creek, skate on
the ice, watch
bunny rabbits,
pheasants, climb
trees and slide
down snow banks.

© David Christy 2003

I wish I could live on
Beaver Creek like the
Kleins, Kelschs and Horners.

When Miss Wells rings the hand bell everyone returns to the school for more front of the room class recitals.

My sister, Mary and Helen Kuhn recite poems.

I'm afraid Mary may get stuck and I almost cry.

Joe Horner spells Chicago and
Miss Wells pats him on the shoulder.

Next there is the last recess period for games

and fresh air and then the final class sessions.

I go to the blackboard to write 1,2,3,4,
and get all the way to 12.

Miss Wells pats my shoulder and I sit down.

At the end of the day I gather my 4 cent tablet
and penny pencil and school things.

© David Christy 2003

Tootsy and Dave love to run home.

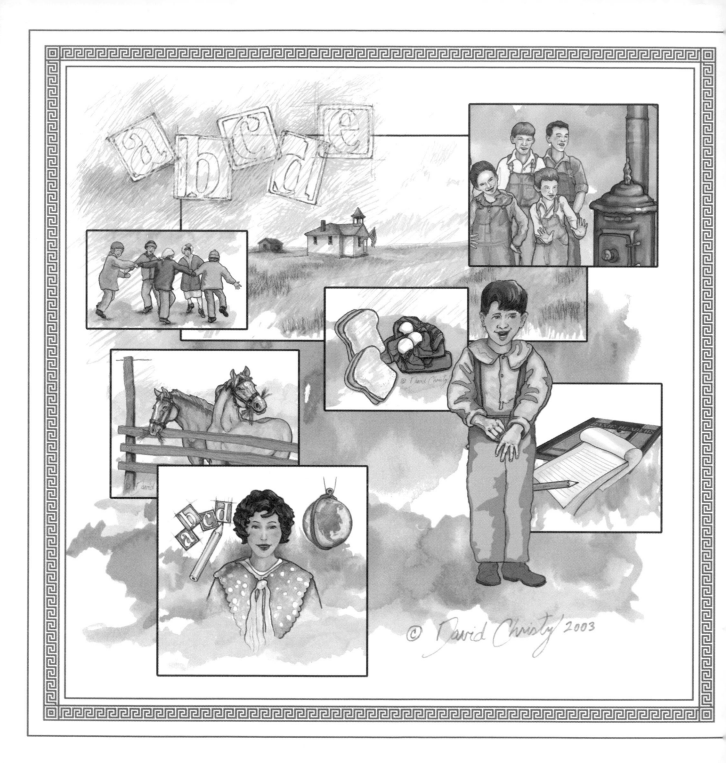

I can't wait to tell about the day
to my mother and father.

# My First Grade, 1932

At my Strasburg, North Dakota rural school in 1932, Miss Wells, the slender, dark, pretty teacher with a spit curl crossing her forehead, says I can start school at age 5, because I have sisters and brothers: Frank, Debert, Wilma and Mary to watch for me. We drive the three miles in a sled or buggy with Dave and Tootsy.   As we pass through Hagel's farm we pick up Martha, a pretty girl with a light face and light hair.   When we are almost to school we pass through Klein's farm and Maggie, Rose and Joe Klein join our ride.    Klein's mother is my godmother and pays attention to me and encourages Tootsy and Dave and I feel happy...   At school the team has its very own stall in the red barn and eats the hay we sat on.   Joe, John, Helen and Frank Kuhn also come with a team smaller and faster than Dave and Tootsy.   Tony Kelsch rides his pony, Spike.  Jake, Joe and Mary Horner walk their mile unless the weather is too cold, then their older brother, Peter, takes them in a sled.   Joe Vetter walks his half mile to school.   To get warm before classes I gather with all the students around the red hot stove.   The smell of coal, varnish and earlier barn chores permeate the room.   Miss Wells starts the school day by hanging a flag on a little pole against the outside of the school, and then ringing a hand bell.   Singing is the first of the 15 minute class sessions.  "My Country Tis of Thee", "Old Black Joe", "Old MacDonald Had a Farm" and "Carry Me Back To Old Virginie" fill the room.   Class sessions at the front of the room are recitals and teacher talk.   During eighth grade Agriculture I hear about Leghorns, Plymouth Rocks, Guernseys, Holsteins, Percherons and Belgians.    Fifth grade Geography is about Bismarck, North Dakota... Pierre, South Dakota and

Sacramento, California.    I and my first graders:Joe Vetter and Joe Klein say the alphabet and learn words in English.    We had only spoken German at home.    Then it is time for a 15 minute recess and a fox and geese game in the snow.    More classes and then lunch hour follows.    Everyone eats at their desk. Miss Wells has lettuce sandwiches and drinks from a black thermos.    Martha has a blue lunch box and thermos with orange nectar.    She shares bites of her jelly bread and pieces of chicken with me... a welcome complement to my syrup sandwiches from an empty syrup pail. Tony Kelsch enjoys hard boiled eggs and syrup sandwiches.    The Kuhn children have cream with sprinkled sugar sandwiches.    Joe Vetter loves sausages from the night before and plain bread.    The Horner's too have syrup sandwiches.    I watch Mary Horner eat.    She is the prettiest one in school.    During lunch hour I play at Beaver Creek, skate on the ice, watch bunny rabbits, pheasants, climb trees and slide down snow banks.    I wish I could live on Beaver Creek like the Kleins, Kelschs and Horners.    When Miss Wells rings the hand bell everyone returns to the school for more front of the room class recitals.    My sister, Mary and Helen Kuhn recite poems.    I'm afraid Mary may get stuck and I almost cry.    Joe Horner spells Chicago and  Miss Wells pats him on the shoulder.    Next there is the last recess period for games and fresh air and then the final class sessions.    I go to the blackboard to write 1,2,3,4, and get all the way to 12.    Miss Wells pats my shoulder and I sit down.    At the end of the day I gather my 4 cent tablet and penny pencil and school things.    Tootsy and Dave love to run home.    I can't wait to tell about the day to my mother and father.

### "My Mother's Apron"...

"My Mother's Apron" is a story about Dr. Keller's mother and the apron she wore daily on their early prairie farm in the 1930's in Strasburg, North Dakota. Keller creates a compelling image of his mother and her home made apron. Always present with everything his mother did, the apron was more than just a garment to be worn. It was an incredible tool used for a wide variety of tasks. The hard cover, 56 page children's history picture book is 8x8 inches in full color. Artist illustrator, David Christy, paints 28 pictures of Keller's mother with her apron. Christy captures the facial expressions from actual archival photographs of her. Additional anecdotal pictures create a living history of the 1930's farmstead home.

*For ages 1 to 101.  Self published 2001, 56 - 8x8 pages, hardcover, $19.95.  ISBN 0-9660833-5-0*

### "My First World"...

In "My First World" Keller tells of growing up near Strasburg and Linton, North Dakota in the 1930's.  At the time Lawrence Welk was a rising star accordionist from Strasburg. Keller chronicles his German Russian ancestors from Germany to Russia to Strasburg, how they worked the land, attended schools, church, parties, dances during the Great Depression, drought and grasshoppers on the early prairies.  *Self published 1995, large print, 76 - 8½x11 pages, plus 9 pages of maps and pictures, perfectbound paperback, $17.50.  ISBN 0-9660833-0-X*

### "Memory Stories"...

In 95 short vignettes, like "My Mother's Apron", "Horse Power", "Welk is Here", "The Watkins Man", "Prairie Humor", Keller evokes the wholesome, sacrificing spirit of his ancestors in the 1930's on the Dakota prairies, the honorable use of what nature provided and the far-reaching effects of faith.

*Self published 1997, large print, 158 - 8½x11 pages, perfectbound paperback, $17.50.  ISBN 0-9660833-1-8*

### Audio Cassette Book of "Memory Stories"...

90 minute, 33 story cassette tape, read by Earl Ackerman, radio personality, KRRB FM, Dickinson, North Dakota.

*Self published 1998,  $16.00.  ISBN 0-9660833-2-6*

Early
Dakota
Prairie
Series